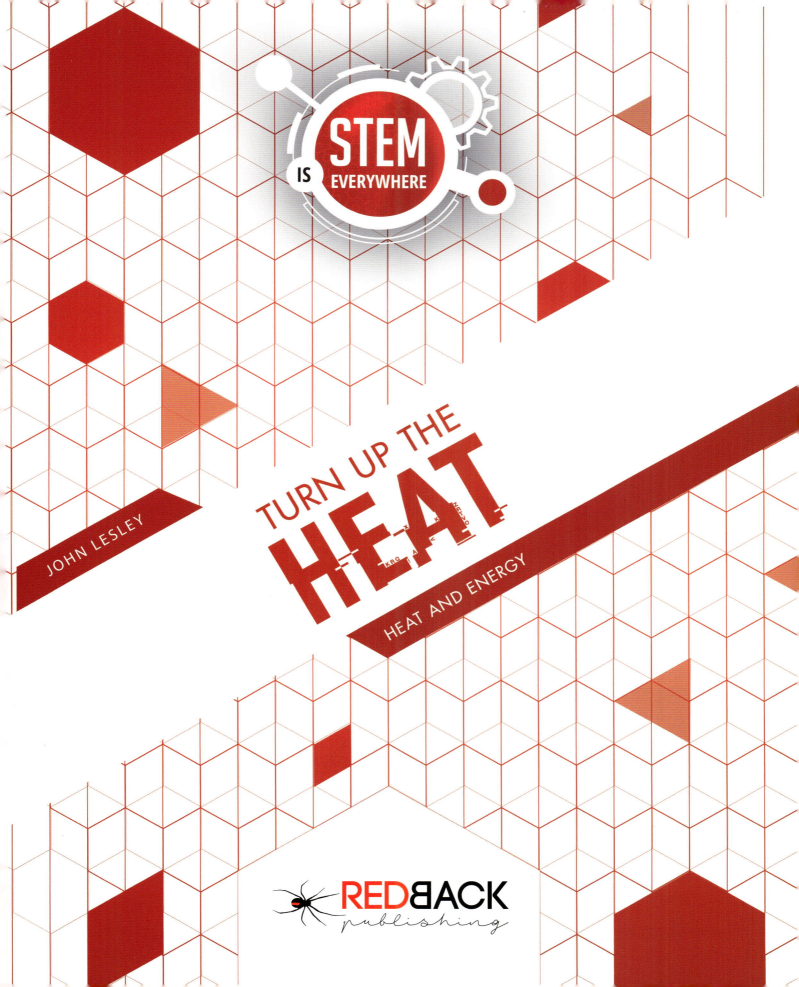

Redback Publishing
PO Box 357 Frenchs Forest NSW 2086
Australia

www.redbackpublishing.com
orders@redbackpublishing.com

© Redback Publishing 2020

ISBN 978-1-925860-88-7

All rights reserved. No part of this publication may be reproduced in any form or by any means (including photocopying or storing it in any medium by electronic means and whether or not transiently or incidentally to some other use of this publication) without the written permission of the copyright owner. Applications for the copyright owner's written permission should be addressed to the publisher.

Author: John Lesley
Editor: Marlene Vaughan
Designer: Redback Publishing

Original illustrations © Redback Publishing 2020
Originated by Redback Publishing

Printed and bound in China

Acknowledgements
Abbreviations: l—left, r—right, b—bottom, t—top, c—centre, m—middle
We would like to thank the following for permission to reproduce photographs: (Images © shutterstock)

Every effort has been made to contact copyright holders of any material reproduced in this book. Any omissions will be rectified in subsequent printings if notice is given to the publisher.

Disclaimer
All the internet addresses (URLs) given in this book were valid at the time of going to press. However, due to the dynamic nature of the internet, some addresses may have changed, or sites may have changed or ceased to exist since publication. While the author and publisher regret any inconvenience this may cause readers, no responsibility for any such changes can be accepted by either the author or the publisher.

A catalogue record for this book is available from the National Library of Australia

CONTENTS

Heat and Energy **4**
Energy Lasts Forever **5**
Thermodynamics **6**
Heat Doing Work **8**
Turning Heat Into Something Else **10**
How Does Heat From a Fire Warm Us? **12**
What Happens During Cooling? **14**
Bigger and Smaller **16**
Taking Charge of Heat **18**
Moving Heat Around **20**
Measuring Heat **22**
Temperature Scales **24**
From Ice to Steam **25**
Burning **26**
Metals and Heat **28**
How Heat Creates Winds **30**
Words About Heat and Energy **31**
Index **32**

HEAT AND ENERGY

The role of heat in the creation of the Universe, human technology and life on Earth is at the centre of all existence.

We may think of heat as something we complain about when the weather is too hot, or the sensation we experience when we are near a fire. This is only a part of the full story, and there is much more to heat and energy than just this.

The transfer of heat between substances is one of the basic ways that energy is used for the development of our technological societies.

ENERGY LASTS FOREVER

Heat is energy. When we use the energy of heat we need to transfer it from one region or thing to another so that it can do work for us.

As things heat up or cool down, it is easy to assume that the energy of heat has just appeared from nowhere and then disappeared.

NO!

One of the basic rules of nature is that energy is conserved. It cannot be made out of nothing and it cannot just disappear. What happens is that energy is transferred to or from something else to cause heating and cooling.

This process is described by a rule that scientists call:

THE LAW OF CONSERVATION OF ENERGY

THERMODYNAMICS

Scientists who study the way that heat can be used to do work, and inventors who create technology that uses heat, both use the science of thermodynamics.

HUMANS ARE NOT THE ONLY ANIMALS THAT USE THERMODYNAMICS TO MAKE THEIR LIVES MORE COMFORTABLE.

Birds living in polar regions have a heat exchange system in the blood vessels of their feet and legs. This stops them from freezing as they stand on the ice and snow.

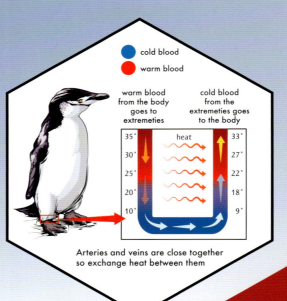

Termites build their mud homes in Australia's hot, northern grasslands under a fierce Sun that could easily dry out their bodies. The interior of the termite mound is designed so that air flows through it, keeping the termites' surroundings at a stable temperature and humidity.

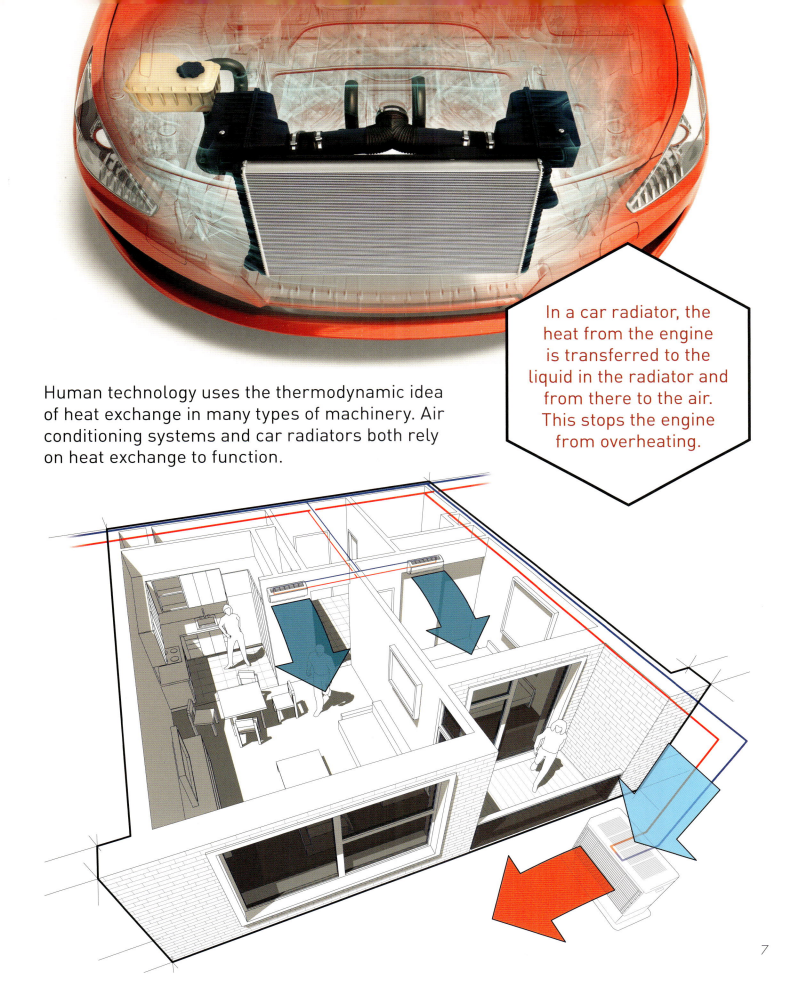

Human technology uses the thermodynamic idea of heat exchange in many types of machinery. Air conditioning systems and car radiators both rely on heat exchange to function.

In a car radiator, the heat from the engine is transferred to the liquid in the radiator and from there to the air. This stops the engine from overheating.

HEAT DOING WORK

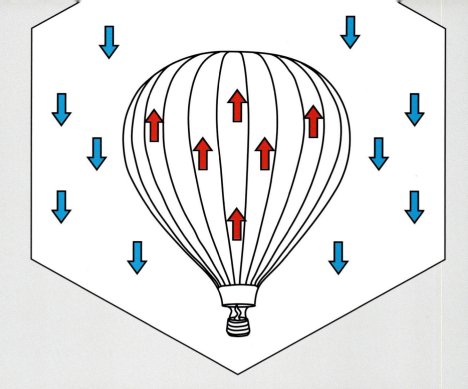

ELECTRICITY GENERATION

Some electricity generators burn coal or gas to make steam that then turns a turbine. This turning motion can be converted into a flow of electricity.

HOT AIR BALLOONS

Hot air balloons use a gas flame to heat air inside a large balloon. Since hot air rises, the balloon also rises into the sky.

MICROWAVE OVENS

Microwave ovens convert the energy of electromagnetic waves into heat for cooking.

STEAM TRAINS

Steam train engines convert the energy stored in coal or wood into steam that moves a train.

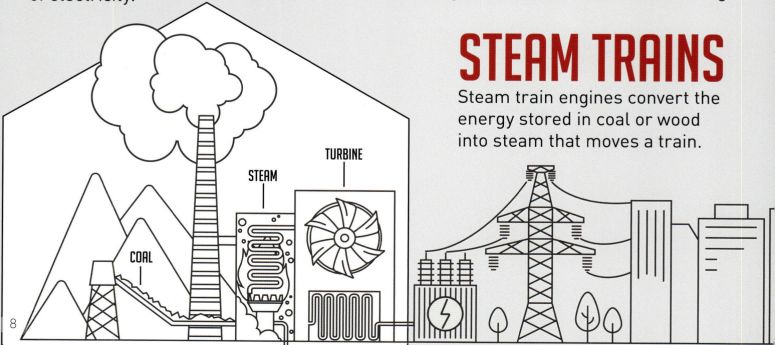

EXERCISE

We feel hot when we do exercise because the burning of carbohydrates by our bodies produces heat.

HAIR DRYERS

Hair dryers use energy from electricity to create heat. The heat is transferred to the air and then blown against hair. Water in the hair evaporates as the heat energy is transferred to it from the hot air.

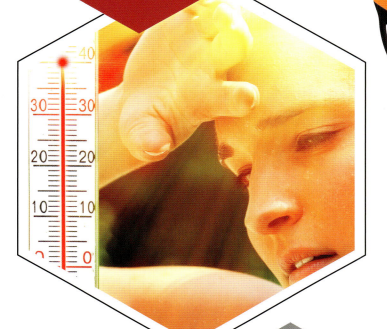

STOVES

The flame of a gas stove transfers energy to a saucepan. The saucepan then transfers energy as heat to the food in order to cook it.

MAKING SALT

Salt farmers use heat from the Sun to drive off the liquid from large pools of salty water. What is left is the white salt we put in our food.

TURNING HEAT ENERGY INTO SOMETHING ELSE

When we use heat to do a job for us, we need to convert it into some other form of energy.

Engineers design machines that convert heat into the energy of movement, which scientists call

KINETIC ENERGY

Motor vehicles, trains and aircraft all have kinetic energy when they are moving.

When the movement causes something to twist rather than travel in a straight line, this type of force is called

TORQUE

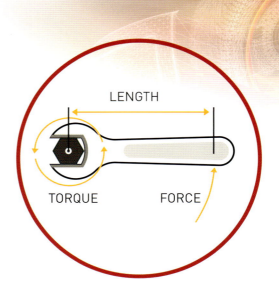

LENGTH

TORQUE   FORCE

MOTOR CARS AND ENERGY

Measuring the torque of a car's engine tells the driver how powerful it is.

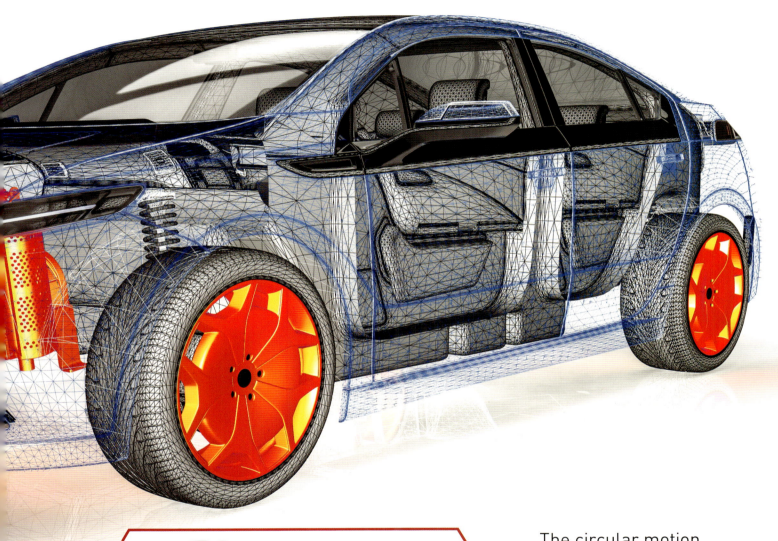

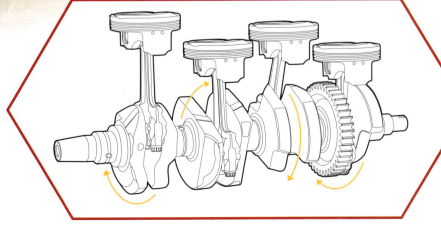

The circular motion produced inside a car engine is converted to straight line or linear motion to make the car move forward. This is the function of wheels, one of humanity's most useful inventions

HOW DOES HEAT FROM A FIRE WARM US?

ATOMS

When a substance gets hot, whether it is a hot stone or our skin, the atoms in the substance are getting *excited*. This is a scientific term that means they start to move around more quickly.

SURPRISING FACT!

The heat from burning wood is coming from the Sun! The tree that grew the wood used sunlight to grow. As we burn the wood, that energy from the Sun is released and turns into heat.

WHAT HAPPENS DURING COOLING?

BLOCKS SEPARATED

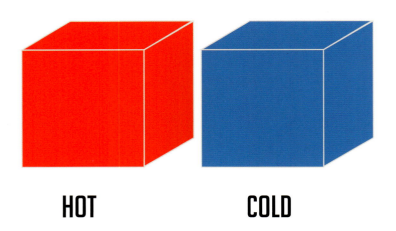

HOT **COLD**

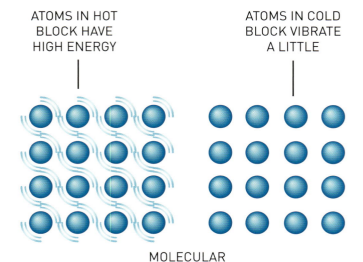

ATOMS IN HOT BLOCK HAVE HIGH ENERGY

ATOMS IN COLD BLOCK VIBRATE A LITTLE

MOLECULAR VIUEW

BLOCKS IN CONTACT

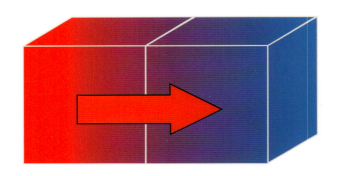

HEAT TRANSFERS FROM WARMER TO COOLER

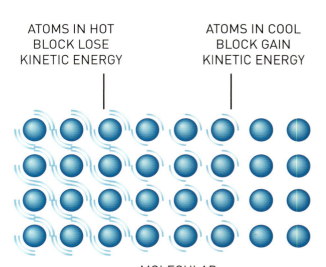

ATOMS IN HOT BLOCK LOSE KINETIC ENERGY

ATOMS IN COOL BLOCK GAIN KINETIC ENERGY

MOLECULAR VIUEW

EXCITABLE ATOMS

The excited atoms in a hot substance calm down and stop moving about as much when the substance cools. The energy of the atoms does not disappear. It moves to a cooler substance whose atoms become a little more active as a result.

NO FURTHER HEAT TRANSFER

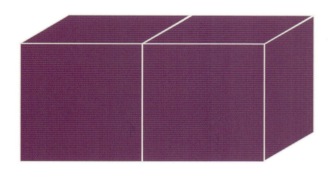

BLOCKS AT SAME TEMPERATURE

KINETIC ENERGY IS SHARED

NO FURTHER HEAT TRANSFER

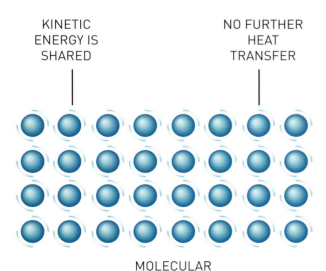

MOLECULAR VIUEW

Heat only moves from a hotter region to a cooler region. Thermal energy cannot flow the other way. When a hot drink cools down, the energy from the atoms in the hot drink moves away into the surroundings.

BIGGER AND SMALLER

TAKING UP MORE SPACE
When we melt a solid, the resulting liquid usually takes up more space. This is because the atoms in the liquid have more energy and are moving around more.

EXPANSION
Adding heat to a substance makes its atoms move around more vigorously. This causes expansion.

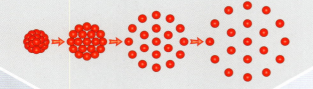

BUT, WHAT ABOUT WATER?

Water is an exception. Its liquid state takes up less space than its solid state, which is ice. This is because the molecules of water form crystals with spaces in them when they turn into ice.

CONTRACTION

Cooling a substance makes its atoms move around less. This causes contraction. Substances usually take up less space as they cool.

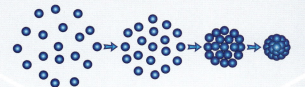

OPENING A JAR LID

Why is it easier to open a tight metal lid on a glass jar after heating it with some hot water?

A

Because the heat expands the metal more than the glass. The lid is then slightly bigger.

TAKING CHARGE OF HEAT

Sometimes we need to stop heat from moving away. If we have a hot drink, we can stop it cooling too quickly by pouring it into a vacuum flask.

The vacuum flask works because it has two layers. Between them is a region where all the air has been taken out, creating a vacuum. Heat cannot travel across a vacuum by conduction and the silvery coating of the flask reduces the amount of radiant heat leaving as well. The result is that the drink inside stays hot.

EMPTY SPACE CREATING VACUUM

CONDUCTORS

Metals feel cool because they are good conductors of heat. They move heat away from where you touch it so quickly that the metal feels cold.

INSULATORS

Rubber, most plastics and wood are not good conductors of heat. This is why they are used on the handles of frying pans. We can pick up the pan, even if it has been sitting on a hot stove, because the non-metal handle is an insulator.

WARM AIR POCKETS IN FLUFFED UP FEATHERS

AIR IS AN INSULATOR

When we wear jackets with feathers or polyester filling in them, we feel warm because the air has been trapped in the fluffy filling. Animals also make use of air as an insulator to keep them warm. When they fluff up their fur or feathers, they are trapping air near their skin. This trapped air acts as a barrier against the cold.

MOVING HEAT AROUND

HEAT ENERGY MOVES THROUGH THE UNIVERSE, AND DOWN HERE ON EARTH, IN THREE WAYS

RADIATION
CONVECTION
CONDUCTION

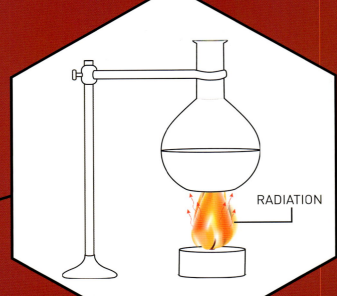
RADIATION

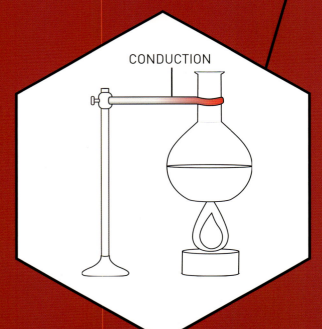
CONDUCTION

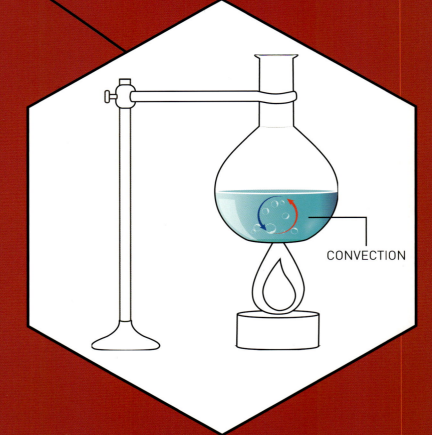
CONVECTION

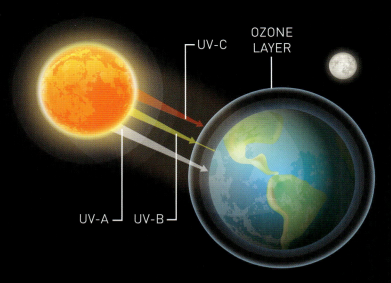

RADIATION
AND THE SUN

Radiation is the way that heat energy travels through the vacuum of space. The energy travels as an electromagnetic wave and does not need matter or atoms for the journey to take place. Radiation is the way heat energy from the Sun reaches us on Earth.

CONVECTION
AND A CUP OF TEA

When heat causes a large amount of matter to move, this creates convection. An example of convection is the movement of the liquid in a hot cup of tea. The heat from the hot water gradually transfers to the air at the surface. This makes the top of the liquid cooler than the part underneath the surface. The cooler liquid starts to fall to the bottom of the cup and is replaced by hotter liquid rising from below. This results in convection currents.

Similar convection currents form in the world's oceans and in the atmosphere.

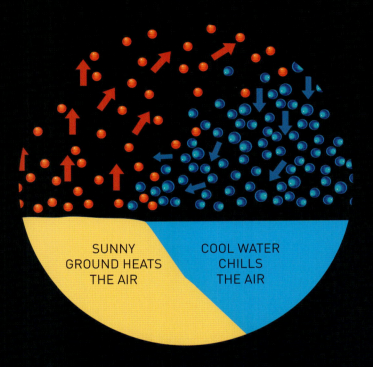

CONDUCTION
AND GETTING BURNT FINGERS

Conduction happens when heat energy is transferred to matter and moves through it, atom to atom. The matter itself does not need to move for the heat energy to get from one place to another. If you touch hot metal, like a saucepan on the stove, you might get burnt as a result of conduction of the heat to your skin.

MEASURING HEAT

Thermometers measure the heat of their surroundings. Inside a thermometer there is a liquid that can expand when it heats up, or contracts when it cools down. As this happens the liquid moves up and down a little tube and we read the value marked on the glass as the temperature. The two liquids most commonly used in thermometers are mercury or coloured alcohol.

Digital thermometers transfer heat from their surroundings to a piece of metal. The digital thermometer measures this and shows the temperature reading on a little display screen.

MERCURY

CALORIES

People on diets need to count their calories. A calorie is a measurement of the heat energy stored in a substance. The higher the calorie content, the more energy there is stored in the food. If a person eats a lot of calories, they need to do exercise or work to turn the calories they have eaten into energy in their bodies. If they do not move around much, the stored energy in their food can turn into fat in their bodies.

1 CALORIE = ENERGY NEEDED TO RAISE THE TEMPERATURE OF 1 GRAM OF WATER BY 1 °C

1 JOULE = 4.2 CALORIES

TEMPERATURE SCALES

THERE ARE THREE MAIN SCALES USED FOR READING A TEMPERATURE MEASUREMENT:

ABSOLUTE ZERO
Absolute Zero is a fascinating concept. In theory, if something could ever reach this temperature, then all the common rules of physics would cease to apply. This is where the realm of quantum physics takes over.

CELSIUS
This scale is based on the boiling and freezing points of plain water.

FAHRENHEIT
This scale is also based on the boiling and freezing points of plain water, but it measures them differently.

KELVIN
0K is the point at which the movement of atoms stops and they have no heat energy. It is also called Absolute Zero.

	Celsius	Fahrenheit	Kelvin
WATER BOILS	100°C	212°F	373 K
WATER FREEZES	0°C	32°F	273 K
ABSOLUTE ZERO	-273°C	-459°F	0 K

FROM ICE TO STEAM

THERE ARE THREE COMMON STATES OF MATTER

These states of matter change as a result of the transfer of heat energy. Even metals can change their state of matter. We normally see metals as hard, solid substances, but they can turn into liquids and even gases if enough heat is applied.

WATER'S THREE STATES OF MATTER
Water as ice will melt into liquid when heat is applied. If we continue to add more heat energy, the liquid turns into steam.

SOLID

LIQUID

GAS

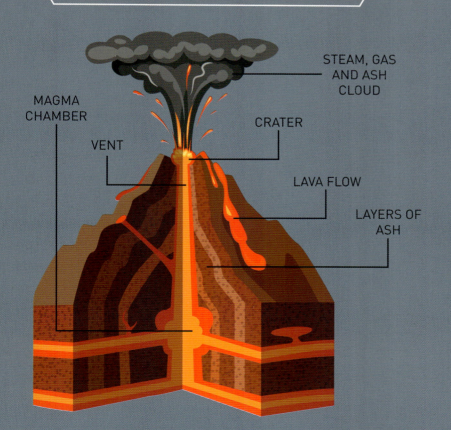

MAGMA CHAMBER
VENT
STEAM, GAS AND ASH CLOUD
CRATER
LAVA FLOW
LAYERS OF ASH

VOLCANOES

The red, flowing lava that comes out of erupting volcanoes is made of rocks in their liquid state. As it cools, the lava turns into solid rocks. The loss of the lava's heat energy has resulted in a change of state from liquid to solid.

BURNING

Burning is one way for energy stored in a substance to be released and to turn into heat.

Burning needs the presence of oxygen. This gas is in the air around us.

To make a fire burn more quickly, we can increase the amount of oxygen around the flames. When we blow on a campfire to make it burn more brightly, we are increasing the amount of oxygen by blowing it out of our own lungs.

FACTS ABOUT FIRE

Fire moves upwards because the gases in the flames are less dense than the air around them.

On a spaceship with no gravity, a fire would form a ball.

FIRE-FIGHTING

As well as starting fires to make use of their energy, we also need to be able to stop fires burning.

WAYS FIRE-FIGHTERS STOP A FIRE BURNING

- They reduce the oxygen supply by smothering the fire with fire-fighting chemicals or sand.
- They place something that will not burn on top of the fire.
- Water can put out a fire by both covering it so no oxygen gets to it, and by reducing the temperature of the burning substance.
- Water may not put out some fires, such as those made by burning oil or by electricity. These sorts of fires can become more dangerous in the presence of water.

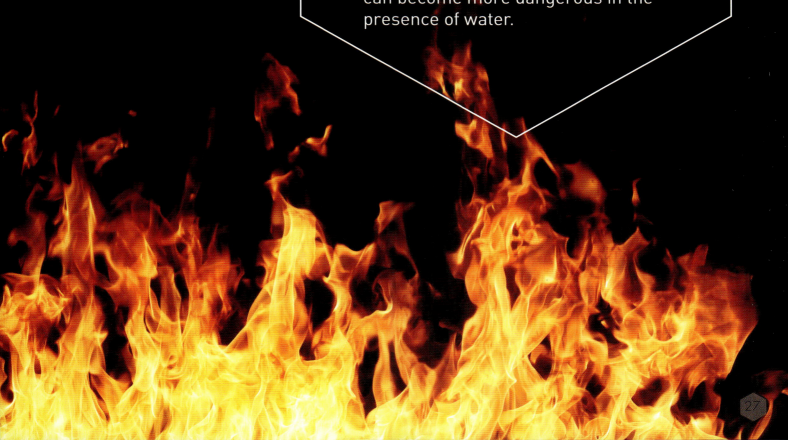

METALS AND HEAT

Heat affects metals by making them expand when they are hot and contract when they get colder.

Since metals are used in buildings, machinery and technology, the behaviour of metals due to heat is an important factor for builders, engineers and inventors to consider.

BRIDGES

Bridge builders place gaps between sections of metal to allow for expansion due to heating by the Sun. Without these gaps the whole bridge could buckle in the heat.

COMPUTERS

The expansion of metal parts inside a computer can cause breaks in electric circuits. The fan inside computers helps to keep the internal parts cool so the computer does not stop working.

ELECTRICITY WIRES

The wires that carry electricity on poles along streets are never hung in stretched, straight lines. This is because the wires need to be able to contract and expand as the weather changes. If they were hung too tightly, contraction in cold weather could make them snap off from their connections.

ENGINEERS AND METALS

Different metals expand and contract by varying amounts. Engineers pick a metal for a particular purpose depending on their knowledge of its ability to withstand extreme heat or cold without moving to a dangerous extent.

METAL ROOFING

Roofs made out of metal roofing can come loose from the building if they expand or contract too much. The metal sheets can bend and the nails holding the roof in place can pop out.

HOW HEAT CREATES WINDS

Where does the wind come from? What is the source of energy on Earth that produces wind? **THE SUN** is the answer to both of these questions.

Heat from the Sun warms large masses of air. As the warm air rises, cooler air takes its place. We feel this as wind blowing.
The movement of air can be in a small area around us, resulting in local breezes. It can also occur over large parts of the land and the oceans, resulting in strong winds and storms.

WIND ENERGY

Since wind is a result of the movement of warm and cold air masses, the wind energy needed to drive windmills comes from the Sun. The Sun is the energy source that causes the air masses to move.

WORDS ABOUT HEAT AND ENERGY

absolute zero	lowest possible temperature
atoms	tiny particles of matter
calorie	measurement of the heat energy stored in a substance
carbohydrates	compounds such as sugar and starch
contraction	getting smaller
convection	movement of heat in liquids and gases
expansion	getting bigger
heat conduction	movement of heat from atom to atom
heat insulator	material that does not conduct heat
humidity	amount of water vapour in the air
joule	1 joule equals about 4 calories
kinetic energy	energy of a moving object
lava	molten rock erupting from a volcano
linear motion	movement in a straight line
oxygen	gas in the atmosphere around us
quantum physics	science of the way subatomic particles move
radiation	movement of energy by electromagnetic waves
thermodynamics	science of heat, work and energy
torque	form of energy that causes twisting
vacuum	place with no air

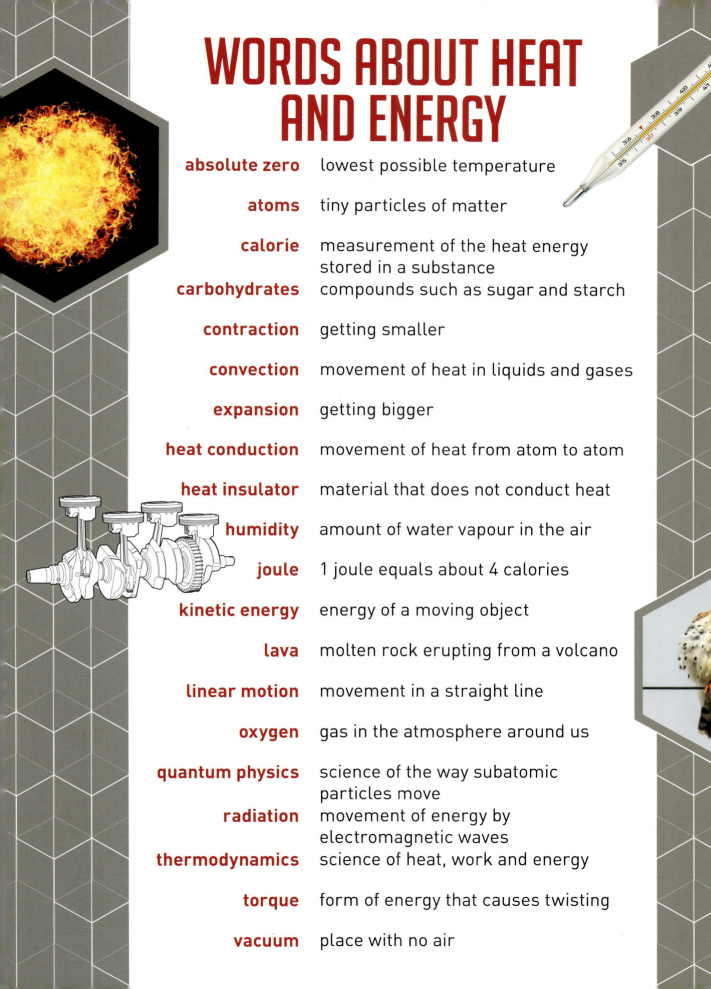

INDEX

absolute zero	23	microwaves	8
atoms	12, 14, 20	motor cars	7
calorie	23	radiation	20
carbohydrates	9	salt farming	9
Celsius scale	24	states of matter	25
computers	30	steam	8
conservation of energy	5	termites	6
contraction	17	thermometer	22
convection	21	torque	10, 11
electricity	8, 9, 30	vacuum	18, 20
expansion	16, 17	water	16, 24
Fahrenheit scale	24	wheels	11
Fire-fighting	26	windmills	28
heat conductor	18, 22		
heat exchange	6		
heat insulator	18		
joule	23		
Kelvin scale	24		
kinetic energy	10